EVERYDAY CODING__

BREAKING DOWN TASKS

Using Decomposition

Elizabeth Schmermund

Cavendish
Square
New York

Published in 2018 by Cavendish Square Publishing, LLC
243 5th Avenue, Suite 136, New York, NY 10016

Copyright © 2018 by Cavendish Square Publishing, LLC

First Edition

Website: cavendishsq.com

This publication represents the opinions and views of the author based on his or her personal experience, knowledge, and research. The information in this book serves as a general guide only. The author and publisher have used their best efforts in preparing this book and disclaim liability rising directly or indirectly from the use and application of this book.

All websites were available and accurate when this book was sent to press.

Library of Congress Cataloging-in-Publication Data

Names: Schmermund, Elizabeth, author.
Title: Breaking down tasks: using decomposition / Elizabeth Schmermund.
Description: New York : Cavendish Square Publishing, 2018. | Series: Everyday coding
| Includes bibliographic references and index. | Audience: Grades 2-6.
Identifiers: ISBN 9781502629784 (library bound) | ISBN 9781502629760 (pbk.) |
ISBN 9781502629777 (6 pack) |ISBN 9781502629791 (ebook)
Subjects: LCSH: Computer programming--Juvenile literature.
Classification: LCC QA76.52 C36 2018 | DDC 005.1--dc23

Editorial Director: David McNamara
Editor: Caitlyn Miller
Copy Editor: Nathan Heidelberger
Associate Art Director: Amy Greenan
Designer: Christina Shults
Production Coordinator: Karol Szymczuk
Photo Research: J8 Media

The photographs in this book are used by permission and through the courtesy of:
Photo credits: Cover Hero Images/Getty Images; p. 4 Matt Benoit/Shutterstock.com; p. 8 (Left) Robert Niedring/Alamy Stock Photo, (Right) Maskot/Getty Images; p. 9 Loftflow/Shutterstock.com; p. 10 Food and Love/Shutterstock.com; p. 11 Patrick He Agency/E+/Getty Images; p. 13 Sebastian/Wikimedia Commons/File:Factor Tree of 8 (Completed).png/ Public Domain; p. 14 Monkey Business Images/Shutterstock.com; p. 16 Light Field Studios/Shutterstock.com; p. 17 People Images/Digital Vision/Getty Images; p. 18 Speed Kingz/Shutterstock.com; p. 19 Only Zoia/Shutterstock.com; p. 20 Ciaran Griffin/Stockbyte/Thinkstock.com; p. 22 Melody Smart/Shutterstock.com; p. 23 CCI/Bridgeman Images; p. 24 DnD Project/Shutterstock.com; p. 25 Syda Productions/Shutterstock.com; p. 26 Vchal/Shutterstock.com.

Printed in the United States of America

TABLE OF CONTENTS __

Understanding Decomposition

Maybe your family celebrates holidays or birthdays with a cake. To bake a cake, you need a recipe. A recipe breaks down the process of making that cake. The first part of a recipe is an ingredient list. It tells you how much sugar you need. It tells you how many eggs you need, too. Next, the recipe tells you how to use those

---

Opposite: In some ways, decomposition is similar to using a recipe to bake a cake.

ingredients. A recipe is just like a process used in **coding**. This process is called **decomposition**.

"Decomposition" sounds like a hard word. But it really just means "breaking things down." It means making something complicated into something simple. A recipe for a cake breaks a big project into ingredients and steps. But decomposition isn't just for cakes or coding. We use it every day in all kinds of ways!

CHAPTER 01

A Closer Look at Decomposition

Sometimes your bedroom gets messy. There are clean clothes on the floor. There are toys everywhere. And the carpet needs to be vacuumed. It can be hard to decide what to do first! This is how computer programmers can feel about big projects.

To clean your room, you decide that you'll fold your clothes first. Then, you put your toys where they belong. Finally, you vacuum. You've just made a plan to break down a big project. Instead

Folding clothes and vacuuming are two of the smaller steps you take to clean your room.

of one big project, you had three small projects. The end result is a clean room.

When computer programmers break down a big project, they end up with a great **program**!

Sometimes people say decomposition is the "**divide and conquer**" rule. Coders divide up parts of their project to meet their goal. They make sure that these parts will fit together

Computer programmers often divide a big project into different parts.

later. They have some good reasons for using decomposition.

First, decomposition saves a lot of time. Sometimes code has mistakes in it. These mistakes are called bugs. They make it so a program can't run like it's supposed to. It can be difficult to find the bugs in code. But imagine if a lot of code is broken down into small chunks.

It's easier to see a mistake in one of these small chunks.

Second, decomposition helps coders to reuse code in new places. It's kind of like a Lego set. You can use the wheels from one kit in another kit to

The code for a timer can be reused over and over.

build something cool. Computer code is like this, too, at times. That's why decomposition is great. A small chunk of code might have a specific purpose. Maybe an **app** needs to have a timer. Coders might have written code for a timer in

Part of every chore or project is deciding who will work on what.

another project. Lucky for them, they can use what they wrote already!

Third, coders can **delegate** a job to someone else. This means they can assign that job to another member of the team. Really big coding projects aren't done by just one person. You might have to clean your messy room by yourself. But what if you could get friends to help? What if one of your friends can fold clothes faster than you can? It would be a good idea to delegate folding to him. This is how coders think. They pick the best person for a particular job. Of course, they have to break the job down first. This is why decomposition is so important. Every big job is actually many small jobs. Decomposition is a way of thinking. It helps us plan. It also helps us work faster and smarter.

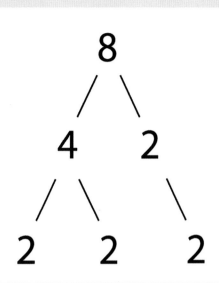

This is an example of a factor tree. The number 8 can be broken down to 4 × 2 or 2 × 2 × 2.

Factoring

Decomposition has another name. It is also known as **factoring**. "Factoring" is a word used in math. It means splitting a math problem into parts in a specific way. Together, those parts make a whole. It is easy to see why decomposition goes by this name, too. Both words talk about breaking things down.

CHAPTER 02

Decomposition in Everyday Life

Decomposition is a skill that all of us use as soon as we wake up. It's how our brains work. We're always solving complicated problems. Think about the first thing you do when your alarm goes off. You make a plan for how you'll get ready for school. It might look like this:

Opposite: You use decomposition every day, such as when you get ready for school.

Packing your backpack is just one task that's part of getting ready for school.

- First, I need to eat my breakfast.
- Then, I need to brush my teeth and wash my face.
- Then, I have to get changed.
- Next, I have to make sure my backpack is packed. I need all of my homework.
- Finally, I need to make sure I get on the bus on time.

You keep using decomposition during the day. Your stomach grumbles at lunchtime. It's telling

Packing a lunch is another important task, and one that many students complete each morning.

you that you are hungry. This is your complex problem. Now you have to decide how to solve this problem. Are you at home or outside? Is there food in your refrigerator? Or do you need to go out and pick up something? What do you feel like eating? What would be a healthy choice for lunch? Do you have enough money to pay for lunch at a restaurant? You might not even realize you're thinking about so many questions. Yet this is how you reach your final decision.

Every song is made of many parts.

Hearing Decomposition

Listen to your favorite song. It sounds like a perfect whole. Actually, it is made up of many different parts. Write down all of the parts of your favorite song: Is there a piano part? A percussion part? Different vocals? A guitar and bass part? All these different musical parts come together to make up a catchy tune. Decomposition is how musicians perfect each part of a song.

Decomposition isn't just used for school and chores. It comes up as we play, too. Think about completing a puzzle. You can't pour all the pieces out of the box and dive right in. You need to make sure the picture is facing up. Some people like to organize pieces by color. A lot of times

people do puzzles together. Then, you have to delegate jobs. Maybe someone works on the frame. Another person flips all the pieces. Or maybe you decide to take sections

When you organize puzzle pieces, you are using a form of decomposition.

of the puzzle. This is a great way to think about how computer code is written. It is exactly like planning to do a puzzle with friends.

CHAPTER 03

Bringing It All Together

We now know that decomposition is a way of thinking. For a computer programmer, decomposition is part of something called **computational thinking**. This is the kind of thinking that states both a problem and a solution in a particular way. The goal is that a human or a computer could carry out steps or **tasks**. Computers understand the world—their **input**—

Opposite: Decomposition is a way of thinking. It's called computational thinking.

Code gives computers instructions to follow.

different ways than humans. Computers need clear instructions to follow. They are not good at creative thinking. Coders make sure computers don't need to make guesses.

Computer code is like the bread crumbs in the story of Hansel and Gretel. Hansel and Gretel use the bread crumbs to find their way. They want to get out of the forest. Code provides the steps

Code is like the bread crumbs that Hansel and Gretel followed.

computers take. But to write this code, coders must use decomposition. They need to break down big problems into small steps. This way, they know what their code should say.

Now let's see how a computer programmer would use decomposition. A programmer named Kat wants to develop a new and exciting app. It's a game that she thinks most of her friends will enjoy. To build this game, she first needs to think through the steps. Then, she can reach her goal.

- First, Kat needs to think about the **function** of her app. What will it do? What kind of game is it?

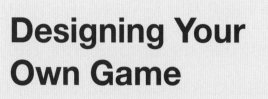

You can write code to create an app or game.

Designing Your Own Game

Thinking about designing your own computer game can be very exciting. Before beginning, you might want to think about these questions:

- What kind of character will you create?
- What is the main goal of the game?
- What is the scoring system?
- What obstacles or enemies will your main character encounter?

If you are writing code for a big project, you might want to delegate some tasks to friends.

- Next, Kat needs to create **graphics** for her app. What will the app look like? This is a task that Kat can do herself, or she can delegate.
- Kat needs to create the step-by-step code and program each part of the app.
- When Kat finishes the graphics and **programming** for her app, she needs to test it. This is how she makes sure it works. It's a good idea to get a friend or a group

It's important to look for mistakes, or bugs, in code.

of friends to test it with her and see what they think about it.

- Based on the testing, Kat can now "**debug**" her app. She can fix anything that is wrong. She can also add improvements based on the suggestions of others.

After following all of these steps, Kat is ready to release her app! She broke down this complex task. Decomposition helped her achieve her goal.

Like Kat, you can use decomposition to create your own computer programs. You can also use decomposition to solve other kinds of complex problems. You already do!

GLOSSARY

app A small program.

coding The process of writing instructions for a computer to follow.

computational thinking Thinking about ways computers can follow instructions to solve a problem.

debug To find and fix problems with computers or computer programming.

decomposition To break down something big into more manageable tasks.

delegate To assign someone a task.

"divide and conquer" Another term for decomposition. A phrase that means splitting up a task so that it's easier to do.

factoring A kind of decomposition done in math.

function The reason or purpose for something.

graphics The pictures and videos we see in a computer game.

input Data that is put into a computer.

program Instructions to make the computer carry out certain tasks.

programming The process of writing computer programs.

task A piece of work to be done.

Books

Lyons, Heather, and Elizabeth Tweedale.

Learn to Program. Kids Get Coding. Minneapolis:

Lerner Classroom, 2016.

McCue, Camille. *Coding for Kids for Dummies*. Hoboken,

NJ: For Dummies, 2014.

Websites

BBC Bitesize: What is Decomposition?

http://www.bbc.co.uk/guides/z8ngr82

This BBC website offers a lesson on decomposition.

Codecademy

https://www.codecademy.com

Learn the basics of coding for free!

INDEX

Page numbers in **boldface** are illustrations.

Elizabeth Schmermund is an author who enjoys writing books for children and teens. She uses decomposition in her daily life to get through the day, whether that's writing a book, building a website, or figuring out how to get her son to school on time.